The Life You've Always Dreamed Of

The Life You've Always Dreamed Of

HOW TO ACHIEVE YOUR AUTHENTIC SELF

Emma L. Westwood

Contents

Prologue:
A Wider Perspective

We are spiritual beings, living on this physical plane in order to experience, to learn, and to grow. We exist, however, in an era of almost mind-boggling contradictions. On the one hand, we are repeatedly told that anything that we desire is within our reach, if only we want it badly enough; we need only think a certain way, and the universe will reward us by dropping it in our lap. On the other hand, even a cursory glance at the news of the day reminds us that we live in a world where extreme poverty, unspeakable violence, and tragedy are a daily reality for millions. What can we make of this appalling incongruity?

Those who believe in the Christian, Muslim, Jewish, or other monotheistic God may believe that the dreadful disparity in living conditions among humans on Earth is for reasons that we cannot understand. Things are as they have been ordained by God. In the afterlife, however, all will become clear to us, though we now "see through a glass, darkly" (1 Corinthians, 13:12).

There are others who believe that the

circumstances in which we are born and live are a result of random factors alone; luck and nothing else has landed us here in a prosperous and peaceful nation, whereas those living in more precarious circumstances were simply unlucky. People who subscribe to this belief tend to be purely materialist, in that they believe that when our bodies die, *we* die.

I believe that there is evidence of an existence for us beyond this earth-bound one, and that we chose, before our birth, the body we now incarnate and the life we now lead, and that, as we die and are born over and over again, we each time select beforehand the human body and circumstances that we will experience in our next life. This is so that we can experience, from one life to the next, all the richness that life on Earth affords us. The evidence for this has become richer in recent decades, with the advent of the so-called New Age. We have now been presented with numerous cases of past life regression, between-lives regression, and even so-called progression (where future lives are seen); we have read about and heard countless cases of near-death experiences, commonplace now in our advanced medical society, which not only support the view of those believing in a specific God or Gods, but also often seem to point to reincarnation, showing belief both in God and in reincarnation to be compatible; and even cases of *shared* near-death experiences or life reviews, where a perfectly healthy bystander, usually a loved one, shares the experiences of someone crossing to the other side.

While the belief that we choose the lives that we lead can serve to mitigate any guilt that we may feel at our lifestyles, so affluent and safe compared to those in war-torn or economically devastated areas of the world, it should never lead us to forget how fortunate we are, and to remember that we must help others less fortunate than ourselves as much as we possibly can. Volunteering our time or money to worthy causes is one way in which we can share our good fortune with those less fortunate. We must work to develop our sense of oneness with all inhabitants of our planet, which in turn will help promote our own psychological wellbeing - a key component, after all, of happiness and fulfilment.

We must, then, maintain a wider perspective while working to create the lives that we desire. Unfortunately, extreme self-centredness is frequently a feature of self-help programs that encourage us to focus on ourselves and what we desire (usually, greater material wealth). We must remember that we are part of a larger whole, members of this huge and wonderful family that includes not only every other human being, but all other animals – and plants – that we share our planet with. We must do what we can to help where feasible - or at the very least do not harm - and always remember to treat others with respect and kindness. Only then can we hope to achieve the successful, fulfilling, and rewarding lives that we have always dreamed of.

Part One

Making Your Now a Good Place to Be

Chapter 1: Gratitude

Living our lives through a sense of gratitude for all that we have is sometimes difficult, but essential if we are to achieve our highest potential. We live in a media-saturated environment that reminds us at every moment what we do *not* have, be it wealth, beauty, youth, sex, the hottest car or biggest house – in short, we are easily convinced that we live in deprivation. The truth, however, is that we are incredibly fortunate to be living in a time and society where we are truly free to craft the lives that we desire. There are over 7 billion human inhabitants of this planet, and the United Nations tells us that one in nine do not have enough food to eat, that almost half of children under the age of 5 who die do so due to malnutrition, and that hundreds of millions of people live in countries plagued by war, while untold millions more live in constant fear of violence.

An unfortunate truth is that those of us living in relative comfort and security often tend to think of those who do not as not quite like us, especially if they are culturally quite different. This "us versus them" approach is, of course, basic to our species. It reinforces group cohesion and cooperation, and has helped *homo sapiens* survive for the hundreds of thousands of years of its evolution. We all know people who are deeply loyal to their family members and friends, but who seem to lack all empathy for those outside their group, seemingly reacting with indifference to their pain, or with envy to their happiness.

We must consciously work towards the understanding that as we share the planet with all members of our species and those of other species, we must feel the same empathy and compassion for strangers as we do for our nearest and dearest. This was the sentiment that President Kennedy was appealing to when he stated, "*Ich bin ein Berliner*," or, in the wake of the recent attacks in Paris, why "*Je suis Charlie*" became a world-wide catchphrase. It should not, however, take a crisis to call up feelings of empathy toward our fellow human beings; we need to keep in mind as we go about our day-to-day lives that we are all in this together.

It is in the spirit of empathy and compassion that we must learn to live with gratitude for all the blessings in our lives. We cannot hope to live the lives that we desire – whether this involves artistic expression, material wealth, good health, meaningful work, loving relationships, or anything else that might make our journey here on Earth worthwhile – if we do not always keep in mind that we must be grateful for that which we have right at this moment.

What if we are suffering through a terrible illness or some great loss? How is it possible to feel gratitude then?

We must place our faith in the wisdom of the universe, and of the Source which is the origin of all consciousness. We must trust that there is a higher purpose, one that may seem obscure to us while we are in the midst of our suffering, but that will one day become clear to us. There are, of course, those who claim that there is no higher power, that all events and circumstances are random, with no inherent meaning; this materialist view is said to be grounded in science, which, it is claimed, makes no allowance for an existence beyond the physical. In this view, those who suffer illness or loss are simply unfortunate; those who prosper are fortunate. This approach is certainly scientific, in the sense that science as we understand it at present cannot describe consciousness, or the afterlife, or the sense of peace and unity that we experience while deep in meditation. However, the limitations of this view are not those of science, but those of the scientific knowledge currently available to us. We are told that quantum physicists shudder when New Age practitioners use the language of quantum physics to describe the spiritual realm, but they must remember that quantum physics and its language belong to all of us, not only to quantum physicists, and that the principles underlying this hard science are often so astonishing that in many respects they do, in fact, straddle the realms of both the physical and the spiritual.

Despite any losses we may experience, or any negative circumstances in our lives that we believe are grossly unfair or undeserved, harboring resentment toward others, or indeed the universe, harms not only those around us but most particularly ourselves. We are all familiar with the fact that by thinking negative thoughts we harm our health; chronic anger and envy raise our level of stress hormones – sometimes called the "flight or fight" hormones - which impact many of our body's systems, including respiratory, endocrine, and circulatory. In a moment of acute danger - when we must run for our lives out of a burning building, for example – certainly the fight or flight response can be a lifesaver, and we have evolved to react in this way to danger for good reason; but constant, low-level stress brought on by simmering resentment or anger is hugely damaging to our bodies, and to our psychological wellbeing and that of the people around us.

There are many strategies that we can employ to place us in a frame of mind that will help us cultivate gratitude. The most effective involve spending time on our own, away from the many distractions that constantly bombard us – television, friends, family, and the countless social media modalities that make huge demands on our time.

Meditation

Meditation is one of the oldest methods known to us for calming the mind and rejuvenating the spirit. It provides us with a much-needed place of serenity away from the demands of a busy day, reconnecting us with the universal consciousness from which we spring, and of which we are a part.

Seasoned meditators can easily slide into that calm space, but even beginning meditators can benefit greatly from the practice. There are no hard and fast rules as to when, where, how often, or even how to meditate; these are up to the individual's inclination and temperament. The resources available to guide the beginner in his or her practice are plentiful, and span all religious and even non-religious persuasions. Many beginners will experiment with various types of meditation – Zen, vipassana, mindfulness, and so on; others will simply create their own. While at first it may seem daunting to sit with eyes closed (or open – Zen meditators, for example, will meditate with their eyes open, and, like much else about meditation, to sit with eyes open or closed is a personal choice) and attempt to clear our minds of thought, there are techniques that can help us in this. The best-known is probably the *mantra*, a word or group of words that we repeat silently to ourselves. Another common technique is that of following the breath, or focusing on the breath to the exclusion of all else. When thoughts intrude – and it is inevitable that they will do so – we can use *labelling*, or naming the thought for what it is; we can simply say to ourselves, "thinking," thus looking at it objectively, as something outside of ourselves, and more easily letting it go. We can also use visualization as we meditate – visualizing, as we breathe in, that we are breathing in the energy of the universe, and as we breathe out, that we make our contribution to that universal energy and thus become one with it.

The benefits of a meditation practice are well-known. They include lowered stress levels, a more balanced mood, better sleep, and even a happier outlook. All of these can help us cultivate our feelings of gratitude, not only for being alive, but for being a part of the cosmic whole.

Recognition of the good things in our lives

Sometimes we lose sight of the positive things that we have been blessed with, focusing instead on what is lacking in our lives. It is a useful exercise to reflect on these blessings; we may, in fact, be surprised at how fortunate we truly are. We may have a job that we enjoy, a loving family, good friends, even an adored pet – all of us have something that we can truly be grateful for. Even those who feel their lives so barren that they seriously attempt suicide but in spite of themselves survive, often do not repeat the attempt, so aware are they of the value of what they came so close to throwing away.

There are various methods that we can employ to remind ourselves of all the good things in our lives. One often suggested strategy is simply to sit with pen and paper, and make a list; another is to sit quietly with eyes closed and picture them one by one. Another is to go for a walk and look around at the signs of the season – snowdrifts in winter, beautifully-coloured trees in autumn – and realize how fortunate we are to be alive, right now, and able to enjoy these gifts of nature.

Sometimes the blessings might be traits that we were born with – intelligence, or artistic talent, or a gift for leadership. These, too, we must be grateful for (without, of course, allowing ourselves to fall into narcissism or conceit). There is truly so much that we have to be grateful for, and we must never lose sight of that fact, even in our darkest hour.

Avoiding toxic entertainment

Our highest-rated television programs and best-selling books are often the least uplifting; our entertainment culture is truly saturated with negativity. We are consistently exposed to reality programming that focuses on the worst of human nature – greed, corruption, and superficiality – and reading material, whether on the internet or in the bookstore, that glorifies selfishness, promiscuity, or the pursuit of wealth and power to the detriment of others. Constant exposure to such material can only lead us to internalize the values that it espouses. In doing so, we grow to believe that our lives are lacking in what we are told are the important things – wealth, sex, youth, beauty.

We must do our best to minimize our consumption of entertainment that does nothing to uplift us, but everything to bring out the worst in us. Envy and greed need not rule our lives; it is possible to control and even eliminate them, but we cannot do so without avoiding exposure to toxic forms of entertainment.

*

There are many ways in which we might remind ourselves throughout the day to practice gratitude. One popular method is to tape a card with a word or two or a short phrase on the refrigerator door or at one's desk at work, or to carry it in one's wallet.

It may at first seem difficult, if not impossible, to cultivate a sense of gratitude, especially if we feel that we have little to be grateful for. However, with practice, attention, and a few simple strategies, though difficult at first, it will eventually become second nature. Gratitude is an essential component in our journey toward effecting a true transformation of our lives.

Chapter 2: Acceptance and Forgiveness

Together with gratitude, we must learn acceptance. There will always be things that we cannot change about ourselves, our circumstances, or the people in our lives; some are obvious, such as our age, our past history, or the death of a loved one. Others may be less obvious, but just as immutable. We may wish that our children or our spouse were smarter or more attractive; we may long for a certain person to reciprocate our feelings of love or of desire. These are things that are outside our control, and acceptance of our powerlessness in these circumstances will do much to diminish our unhappiness.

There is much wisdom in the Serenity Prayer, written by Reinhold Niebuhr in the 1940s and later made popular by Alcoholics Anonymous:

God, grant me the serenity to accept the things I cannot change
The courage to change the things I can
And the wisdom to know the difference.

Letting go of past injuries is perhaps one of the

most difficult aspects of acceptance. This is one instance where acceptance becomes closely linked to forgiveness – and it is at the nexus of acceptance and forgiveness that we find true peace. Certainly, many of us have been grievously injured in our pasts, in ways that might seem unforgivable. This could have involved abandonment, physical or mental cruelty, sexual abuse – the list of possibilities is endless. If this injury occurred in childhood, it is doubly difficult to practice acceptance; children are so vulnerable that any serious injury done them seems truly monstrous, and if we have been victims of such injury, as we reflect upon it we return to that place of vulnerability. We must, though, find a way to accept, to forgive – and, finally, to move beyond the past. But how? Simply determining to forgive those who have injured us, despite our anger toward them, is not enough. Short of seeking professional help – and this should definitely be an option when all else fails – we must employ effective strategies to free ourselves of the bonds of the past, accept what has happened, forgive if necessary, and begin to live life in the present.

Forgiveness is not about the person who did us the injury; it is about ourselves. It is not driven by any outside event; it does not rely on external circumstance; it is not contingent upon the actions or behaviors of other people. Forgiveness is entirely a product of our own hearts and minds.

It can be instructive for any of us struggling with forgiveness to consider instances where people have forgiven acts that many of us would have considered unforgivable. There is perhaps no crime more horrifying than that of the murder of one's child; yet, inconceivable as it may seem, parents of murdered children have forgiven the murderers. In doing so, many have stated that they found a peace and a healing that they never thought possible. If victims of such horrible crimes can put aside feelings of vengeance and hatred, surely we can, as well, when the injury is so much less grievous.

Sometimes it is ourselves whom we cannot forgive for some past wrong. Perhaps we were systematically unkind or did some injury to someone – a parent, sibling, or friend – who has since died and to whom we would dearly love to apologize. Alternately, we may have committed some offense, illegal or otherwise, that no one else is aware of. Whatever it may be, often our own feelings of guilt far exceed any anger or resentment that we may feel toward others.

Whether the challenge is to forgive another, or to forgive ourselves, if we hope to live happy and fulfilled lives we must forgive. Holding onto anger hurts us more than it does anyone else; this is clear. However, it also hurts those closest to us. Children of divorced parents are often damaged emotionally by one parent's feelings of betrayal or of anger toward their spouse; friends and even co-workers will begin to avoid those whose resentment defines their social interactions, or who constantly speak of real or imagined wrongs.

Forgiveness is not easy, and we need to work hard to achieve it. In order to do so, we must first acknowledge that it is a good thing to forgive, letting go of any ideas we may be harbouring that somehow, as the wronged party, we have every right to carry this grudge. We must also recognize – though this is perhaps the most difficult aspect of this very difficult process – that persisting in carrying resentment and hatred toward someone who has injured us is benefiting us in some way. Is playing the victim giving us a kind of attention that we crave? Are others pitying us in a way that we find subconsciously gratifying? Is focusing on some wrong done to us diverting our attention from issues that we would rather not address?

If we hope to achieve a sense of peace and satisfaction in our present, we *must* stop dwelling on the past in a destructive way. There is certainly nothing wrong with reviewing fond memories, or even occasionally remembering unhappy past moments; however, we must learn how to prevent such memories from dominating our thoughts and overtaking us in the present.

One of the most rewarding ways of dealing with past hurt is to acknowledge that all that happens to us is a learning experience. We are, after all, students in the school of life; and without experience, good and bad, we cannot grow as healthy, compassionate beings. Many people who have had near death experiences or who have undergone past life regression confirm that we choose to be born in the circumstances that we find ourselves in. This is not to say that every experience that we undergo is predetermined; nonetheless, it is true that every one of our incarnations here on Earth has its purpose, which is that we continue to develop, to grow, and to learn.

Whether we find ourselves in circumstances of misfortune or those of great joy and prosperity, we must remember that our lives are guided by our own free will, and that we can choose to dwell on past wrongs, wallow in misery, and resent those who seem more fortunate; or we can adopt an attitude of love, of forgiveness, and of gratitude. Studies on happiness have shown that some of the happiest people on Earth are those whom we would deem the most unfortunate – those living in great poverty or ill health, barely able to keep a roof over their heads and food on the table. They have found their happiness in places that we often tend to dismiss or minimize – the love of their families or the closeness of their friendships. Many of these people have been grievously injured in war or by the more powerful in their societies, yet they do not nurture resentment and anger, but choose instead to focus on what is good in their lives.

In short, forgiveness is a choice. We are free-willed beings, and we can decide - regardless of how severe or extreme a wrong has been done to us – to forgive, and to move on. It is unquestionably difficult to accept the past and forgive ourselves or others for past wrongs, but it is essential if we are to craft lives for ourselves that are joyful and rewarding.

Chapter 3: Compassion

There are few practices more life-affirming than that of compassion. When we cultivate compassion, we turn our focus outward, recognizing the unity of all, and our place within the fabric of the cosmos. It is compassion that allows us to experience friendship, love, and intimacy; it is through compassion that we feel empathy, where we feel the suffering of others as though it was our own.

When a natural disaster strikes – an earthquake, tsunami, or volcano – that leads to loss of life, we may be brought to tears by the suffering of the thousands killed or displaced. We imagine what it would be like if we lost *our* homes or families, or all that was familiar and dear to us. This reaction may seem perfectly natural to us; however, there are a few interesting aspects of compassion that may not be readily apparent.

Researchers have discovered that our feelings of compassion are more easily elicited where the victims are more like us. We may dislike recognizing this about ourselves, but it is undeniable. If a war or natural disaster occurs in a country with a population more like ourselves – for instance, a European nation, if we are American – we react far more strongly than we would had it occurred in Asia or Africa. This is why – as has been shown time and again - that the wealthy are, in general, overall less compassionate than the poor; the poor can more readily identify with the unfortunate. It is also an unpleasant fact that we can become somewhat immune to others' suffering when we are constantly bombarded with it, whether on television or in our day-to-day lives (this is known as "compassion fatigue," and it is a reality for many first-line workers in the health care system, or those regularly exposed to war or other crises).

How can we nurture our sense of compassion for others? There are several ways that we can help our feelings of compassion grow.

Learning to forgive

As was discussed in the last chapter, we must learn to forgive others - and ourselves - for past misdeeds, regardless of their gravity. Without forgiveness, we will not get past our feelings of suffering and resentment to allow compassion in.

Feeling compassion for the self

As is the case with forgiveness, it is virtually

impossible to feel compassion for others if we do not feel it for ourselves. This is not whining or self-pity, but a recognition that it is okay not to be perfect. Many judgmental people, who always seem to be pointing out the flaws in others, are actually acutely aware of their own flaws, and continually berate themselves. It is sometimes said of such people that "he's as hard on himself as he is on others": this is not a trait that should be nurtured, but one that needs to be eliminated as much as possible if we hope to grow compassion.

Increasing awareness of the world

We are often so caught up in our day-to-day lives, some of us juggling career, children, partner, and other pursuits, becoming so focused on ourselves, that we neglect to widen our awareness of the world around us. We might say, "I never watch the news, it's too depressing," or "I haven't got time to read the newspaper." We may have a vague sense that there is trouble in some foreign country, perhaps a civil war or famine, but we have no true understanding of the circumstances, and no desire to gain one. This self-centered way of being encourages such a narrow view of the world and our place within it that it allows little space for compassion to grow.

Behaving with civility

A much-overlooked and often much-maligned practice is that of behaving civilly in our interactions with others. Even a casual glance at what is currently trending in social media or reality television makes it obvious that behaving toward others with politeness and respect is frequently deemed laughable, weak, boring, or old-fashioned. Often it seems that the ruder or more shocking the behavior, the more it is applauded. Sometimes we witness back-and-forth retorts, perhaps via Twitter or other social media, between celebrities, though at other times the targets of the behavior are powerless or anonymous, and little thought is given to them. Though the internet certainly has its positive aspects, it also has many negative ones. Trolling, cyberbullying, and other negative behavior engaged in by those hiding behind the anonymity of their computers has become an unfortunate reality in the internet age.

No one deserves to be the target of rudeness. Even when someone is rude to us, we gain nothing, except perhaps a foul mood, by being rude in return. Being polite when interacting with others benefits all parties.

Volunteer

Volunteering in our communities – whether for an hour a day, or an hour a month – is one of the most generous acts that we can engage in. We may not be in a position to give financially, but with volunteering we give of ourselves. Every community has many volunteering opportunities, whether helping at a food bank or homeless shelter, answering telephones for a charitable organization, or even teaching illiterate adults how to read – there is everywhere a great need for people to give their time to others. Volunteering is one way that we can learn to turn our focus from ourselves onto others.

*

It is incontrovertible that without compassion, we cannot lead truly meaningful lives. Focusing only on ourselves and our successes – and failures – may seem natural, but it is ultimately unrewarding. To fully experience what it is to be a happy, healthy human being, we must find pleasure in giving as well as taking, and to give willingly, we must feel compassion for others.

Chapter 4: Engaging In Supportive Relationships

Human beings are social creatures, and it is in many ways our relationships with others – with our family and closest friends, as well as with co-workers, neighbours, or acquaintances – that give us our sense of self-worth and define who we are. There are philosophers who believe that consciousness – the subjective "I" – cannot exist in isolation, but is, in fact, made real only through its interaction with others within human society. Though this view negates the existence of a true self, or soul, that survives the body and exists outside time, it reinforces the importance of our social ties, and how poor our lives would be without them.

All of us are enmeshed in a web of social relationships, some obviously more important than others. Whereas the less important relationships that we engage in – those with the corner grocer, for example, or the neighbour with whom we exchange pleasantries but not much else – may change or end without affecting us unduly (the grocer may leave his shop, or the neighbour move away, and we may never see either again or even think about them again), the more important relationships in our lives have significant effects on not only our psychological wellbeing and emotions, but even on our physical health.

It has been proven time and again that people who live long, healthy lives have close social ties. It is impossible to underestimate the importance of having intimate, nurturing relationships. We do not, of course, all prefer to surround ourselves with large groups of people; many of us prefer to have only a few close friends. A quiet evening with one or two friends may be as rewarding to a more introverted person as attending a party with scores of people may be to the extrovert. What is important is that we indulge our need for close, human contact and social ties.

Toxic relationships

Of course, it is important to recognize that not all our social ties are beneficial to us. Few of us have not found ourselves in what are commonly referred to as "toxic" relationships, where we are left feeling depleted, stressed, or perhaps even depressed. It is normal to hope that our most important relationships will uplift us, so that we feel good about ourselves; we expect to be encouraged and supported by those in whom we confide, and with whom we choose to spend our time. The toxic relationship will often have the opposite effect on us. Such a relationship may be difficult or impossible to change (that with a difficult superior at work, for example), but in many cases we hold the power to alter the dynamic of the relationship, or, if necessary, even end it.

Sometimes it is difficult to step outside a relationship and look at it from an objective distance; we may not, in fact, know that a relationship is having a negative effect on our psychological - and by extension physical - health. If things are not going well, we may blame ourselves (this tends particularly to be the case with respect to romantic relationships). There are, however, a few simple questions that we can ask ourselves about a relationship; our replies can provide clues as to whether or not we are in a toxic situation:

- Can you say "no" to the other person without feeling criticized?

- Do you feel worse, instead of better, after having contact with him or her?

- Does the relationship make you feel depressed?

- Do you feel a lack of support from the other

person?

- Are you always hoping that things will improve?

- Do you blame yourself for what's wrong with the relationship?

- Do you fantasize about the relationship ending? (in a romantic relationship, this may go so far as fantasizing about the death of the other person, or that he or she will meet someone else and leave).

- Do you avoid contact with the other person?

Replying "yes" to any of the above questions should be a warning sign that the relationship is unhealthy. This does not necessarily mean that it is unsalvageable; especially in romantic relationships, ending it may be complicated (especially if there are children involved). A decision to seek counseling, rather than end the relationship, may be a good decision, provided that both partners agree.

Without question, the relationships that we have with others largely define us, giving us our sense of who we are and what our place is in the world. Every close relationship that we have – those with friends, family, and partners – should be supportive. Even during serious arguments or disagreements - which can rarely be avoided in even the healthiest of relationships - we must always feel that, ultimately, we are cared for unconditionally.

Chapter 5: Taking Care of Ourselves Physically

We cannot expect to lead meaningful, rewarding lives if we do not respect ourselves, and in respecting ourselves, we must not forget to respect our bodies. Taking care of ourselves physically is as important as is looking after ourselves emotionally and psychologically. In fact, how we feel physically often has a direct impact on our psychological wellbeing; for example, if we consistently eat foods that are unhealthy and do not nourish and sustain our bodies, we cannot help but feel irritable and out of sorts, and if we tend to overeat, we will gain weight and suffer the many physical and emotional consequences that obesity entails. It furthermore should go without saying that the abuse of drugs or alcohol will impact us negatively in all respects.

Exercise

Exercise is the single most important activity that we can pursue in order to improve not only our overall physical health, but our mental, emotional, and cognitive health, as well. It has been shown time and again in rigorously-designed double-blind studies that exercise outperforms all other lifestyle factors, even diet, in contributing to our wellbeing, both subjective and objective. It not only has a beneficial effect on our mood – helping to fight depression, for example – and our cardiovascular health, flexibility, and weight, but it can also enhance our social lives, as many types of physical exercise are done with others, whether in a gym or class setting or on a court or playing field.

Humans evolved to be physically active. With the exception of the current post-industrial age, for the hundreds of thousands of years that our species has been in existence we have spent most of our waking hours in physical activity, and in many cultures today, that continues to be the case. Unfortunately, as those of us in the Western industrialized world have become less active and have had more and more access to high-calorie, poor-quality food, there has been a concomitant rise in the rates of obesity and of chronic diseases such as type 2 diabetes and hypertension.

It is an unfortunate fact that the less we are active, the less we are inclined to be active; the more active we are, the more energetic we become. Some of us may feel that we have been sedentary for so long that it would be impossible to change. We claim that we "hate exercise," that we "have no time for exercise" (though we seem to find plenty of time to sit in front of the television or surf the internet), that we are too overweight or in too much chronic pain to risk exercise. In fact, there is a form of exercise that is appropriate for everyone, regardless of age, weight, or physical limitations.

The benefits of exercise are so well-established that there really is no credible excuse to avoid it. Though it is true that the most beneficial type of exercise is of the aerobic type – it has proven positive effects on the cardiovascular system, mood, and cognitive function – even low-impact exercise is of benefit. Stretching, yoga, tai-chi, even going for a daily walk – all forms of physical activity have their upside, and if engaged in judiciously to prevent injury, very little downside. (Of course, it goes without saying that any radical change in or adoption of an exercise program should be approved by a doctor, particularly in cases of known illness, chronic disease, or risk factors).

Nutrition

It is an incontrovertible fact that as Western society has become more affluent, the human tendency to prefer sweet, salty, and high-fat food has been exploited by those who are happy to provide us with what we desire, even if it is killing us. The easy availability of inexpensive, processed, nutritionally poor food that nonetheless tastes great (to many of us) is obvious with even a casual glance at any supermarket shelf. It is difficult, too, to look in any direction in any city in North America, in particular, without seeing a fast food restaurant. It is very, very difficult to avoid being tempted by food that is undeniably bad for us. Little wonder that the leading causes of death in North America - heart disease, cancer, and stroke - are greatly impacted by nutrition (though cancer is not necessarily a disease of obesity and poor nutrition, many types of cancers are, in fact, linked to these factors). In fact, while smoking has traditionally been considered the leading cause of preventable death in North America, obesity is rapidly closing in on the top spot.

If we want to live lives that are healthy and productive, we must learn to eat properly. While there is controversy over the role that saturated fat or dietary cholesterol play in chronic illness and obesity, as with many other lifestyle choices, *moderation* is the preferred approach. It is undeniable that red meat consumption carries many risks; but it is also unrealistic to expect a committed steak lover to become vegan to improve his health.

Cutting down on red meat (ideally, to once a week

or less), increasing the consumption of whole foods, minimizing that of processed foods, eating more whole grains, fruits, and vegetables – this is within everyone's reach. Even those who dislike vegetables must recognize that this is a huge category of foods, and there is surely at least one vegetable that even an inveterate vegetable avoider can like. There are, too, countless resources on the internet and in the bookstore that show us how to prepare these foods in novel and very palatable ways.

Sleep

Most of us living the fast-paced Western lifestyle are chronically sleep-deprived. Though we may convince ourselves that we need only five or six hours' sleep per night – and many people get less sleep than that – it is, in fact, true that for most people at least seven hours of sleep per night on a regular basis is essential for good health and optimal mental and emotional functioning.

Though we may tell ourselves after a series of nights of too little sleep that we'll make up for it on the week-end, it is not possible to make up for a regular pattern of lost sleep (what is known as "sleep debt") by occasionally sleeping in. It is essential for most of us that we endeavour to sleep at least seven hours – more, if at all possible –

every night. This would undoubtedly dramatically reduce the need for medications for any number of ills that are perhaps caused, and certainly exacerbated, by lack of sleep. Certainly, depression, anxiety, inability to focus, and even overeating have been linked to chronic sleep deprivation; and it is well-known that sleepiness behind the wheel is a major factor in road accidents (driving while sleepy being comparable to driving while drunk, in terms of attention and reaction times).

One of the more common excuses for sleeping too little is that we do not have the time to sleep a full seven or eight hours; our lives are so busy working and taking care of our families that we simply do not have that extra hour or two to devote to sleep (an excuse commonly used for avoiding exercise, as well). It is instructive to realize that members of the typical North American household watches anywhere from four to seven hours of television *per day*; surely at least some of that television time would be better spent getting the sleep we need.

*

It should be obvious that looking after our bodies is as essential to our overall wellbeing as is ensuring our emotional and psychological health; in fact, when we feel physically unwell, we cannot help but feel emotionally or psychologically depressed. It is important, then, to work toward achieving our optimal level of physical health.

Of course, many of us, despite our best efforts, continue to suffer from chronic conditions; we may sometimes even find ourselves facing a serious or life-threatening illness. In such cases, we must engage fully in the healing process, taking responsibility for our own health, working with our physicians to reach our maximum potential level of wellness. It is not sufficient to simply turn ourselves over to the healthcare system, expecting those professionals to make us well; we must be partners with them in our quest for wellness, finding, if necessary through trial and error, the approaches that we can take to support ourselves through this trying time. This might include meditation, prayer, visualization, or other such contemplative practices; or we may find that being with others in a social setting is more rewarding. What is important is that we play an active role in working toward becoming the healthiest that we can be.

Chapter 6: Finding Meaning in our Work

One challenge that many of us face is that of finding meaning in our work. Though some of us are fortunate enough to have careers that we love and jobs that we adore, it is an unfortunate fact that many of us get up every morning and go to jobs that we would not hesitate to leave if we won the lottery or inherited a substantial amount of money.

We spend the better part of our productive lives at work; it thus makes little sense to talk of finding joy and meaning in life if we feel depressed or frustrated in our day-to-day work lives.

For some of us, the option of leaving an unsatisfying job to find something more suited to our temperament or lifestyle exists, but for many of us, it does not. In some areas – particularly large cosmopolitan cities – there may be many choices for the average job-seeker, but in smaller towns or more economically depressed areas, this may not be an option. It may also be impossible for other reasons – age, health, or skill level – to consider leaving a current job to seek another.

We may thus find ourselves working simply to keep a roof over our heads or food on the table; working not because we enjoy our work, but because we feel that we have no choice but to do the work that we are doing. We may even dislike our jobs to the extent that we feel depressed every morning, or suffer from an extreme case of the "Sunday night blues." Even in such circumstances, however, you can employ certain strategies to increase your satisfaction with your work, and find meaning in what you do.

Change your attitude toward your work

This sounds obvious, but it is one of the keys to finding greater satisfaction in what we do. We all know of two people who find themselves in similar circumstances – suffering from a serious illness, perhaps, or the end of a relationship – who nevertheless react quite differently, one with resilience and a determination to improve his circumstances, and the other by complaining continuously, becoming depressed, or giving up. Though their external circumstances may be very similar, it is their attitudes toward these circumstances that makes the difference.

One approach to changing your attitude toward your job – even if you dislike it or find it boring or unrewarding – is to look at the bigger picture.

What role does your work have in the overall function of the organization? Taking a step back and examining the way that your position fits into the overall operation of the company that employs you can help you understand that all jobs are important, from that of CEO to that of the people who keep the workplace clean.

Another effective strategy is to honestly evaluate all components of your job. You may dislike typing, for example, yet spend a large part of your day typing; or you may need to spend long hours on the telephone dealing with unhappy customers, which you find depressing or stressful. One way of dealing with this is to spend one day making a list of every single task that you perform, and indicating how much time you spend on each. You will probably be surprised to find that there are features of the job that you, in fact, enjoy, and that you spend far more time on these tasks than you had realized. This strategy can also help you organize your time in such a way that you spend more of it doing what you enjoy, and less doing what you dislike.

You may also find that though the job itself is not terribly interesting, you enjoy the company of your co-workers, or look forward to your lunchtime or break-time activities.

Make use of your commute

You may be among the fortunate who have a very short commute, walking or perhaps biking to work. Most of us, however, find ourselves battling rush hour traffic in our cars or standing on crowded buses or trains for an hour or more every day. Though the commute is traditionally considered an unwelcome necessity and is regarded as wasted time that could be spent in more fruitful pursuits, it is possible to make one's daily commute not only more pleasant, but even fruitful and rewarding.

There are many ways that you can make your commute an enjoyable one, or even one of the highlights of your day. If you drive to work, you can consider turning off the radio (morning radio is notoriously loud, raucous, and even stress-inducing) and instead listen to a CD of your favourite music, or an audiobook. If you commute via public transportation, you can choose to read, listen to music or a podcast, or even meditate. Whether driving or using public transportation, you might consider availing yourself of the many courses now available on CD or via digital download from companies such as The Teaching Company (where college-level courses covering every conceivable subject, from mathematics and the sciences to English literature and art appreciation, can be purchased).

Consider expanding your group of work friends

Most of us will have a few friends at work, with whom we have lunch, take our breaks, or discuss our personal lives. These work friendships become part of the background routine of our lives. You may have one or more colleagues whom you say "hello" to, but never had a conversation with. This may be because they work in a different department, or hold a position at a different level than yours (we do tend to gravitate toward those who hold similar positions in the company hierarchy), or for reasons that are not entirely clear to you. Why not consider striking up a conversation with a co-worker whom you know only casually? You may discover that you have more in common than you thought.

Avoid malicious gossip

Gossip has been recognized as an important factor in social interactions, especially in the work environment, operating as a social glue and fostering a feeling of belonging to an "in-group." For these and other reasons, gossip is not, in and of itself, necessarily a bad thing; but one would do well to steer clear of the more overtly malicious or hurtful gossip. Gossiping about a certain manager's unfair treatment of employees is one thing; criticizing her for being physically unattractive is another. Engaging in malicious gossip not only injures the person who is its target, but it harms the reputation of those participating in it. It leads to hurt feelings and an unpleasant atmosphere.

Make your work space as pleasant as possible

Whether you have only a tiny cubicle and desk, or whether a spacious corner office with private bathroom, making your work space as pleasing as possible to you is well within your ability. You probably cannot change the computer, telephone, printer, or other office equipment that you have to work with; but you can bring in photos of your loved ones or pets, or small decorations or other knickknacks that you enjoy having around you. If you love plants or flowers, you may decide to bring in a favourite plant or occasionally pick up flowers on your way to work to place on your desk. You may be an animal lover; why not pick up a page-a-day calendar featuring a different animal photo each day? There are truly endless possibilities for making your work space one that you can enjoy walking into every morning.

*

We spend so much of our lives at work that it only makes sense to focus on making that time as productive and enjoyable as possible. The key is to realize that it is within our power to change our mood, and our feelings. Even if we dislike our jobs, finding them monotonous, unfulfilling, or demeaning, it is within our power to change our attitude toward our work, and decrease our feelings of dissatisfaction or resentment. After all, if we persist in wallowing in anger and self-pity, we will do nothing but continue to harm ourselves and those loved ones who are most affected by our feelings and behaviors.

Chapter 7: Realize That it's Never Too Late

Most of us are expected to decide on our life's path at a very young age; teenagers go to college, having been pressured into choosing a major and thus locking themselves into a career path that they may one day realize was the wrong one for them. Others, for financial or other reasons, do not go to college, or may even decide not to complete their high school education. In most cases, the teenager or young adult has already made the decisions that will shape the several decades of work - and life – that lie ahead.

Most of us can expect to live well into our 80s and beyond. We used to think of 40-year-olds as "middle-aged;" that has changed, as the many options available to most North Americans in terms of health and lifestyle activities have led to the popular concept of 40 being "the new 30," 50 being "the new 40," and so on. We look back on our parents' and grandparents' generations, marveling at how old they seemed even at 35 or 40, and congratulate ourselves on having maintained our youthful appearance and joie-devivre well beyond that age. Does it stand to reason, then, that despite our dissatisfaction with our jobs, our leisure activities, our lives, we feel that it is "too late" for us to change those circumstances? Why should we believe that the dreams we held as young people must be forgotten and buried, to add to our list of regrets when it really *is* too late?

Be realistic

Though it is never too late to make a positive change in your life, and to pursue the lifelong dreams that you thought would never be realized, it is important to be realistic. If you had always dreamed of being a ballet dancer, but have never studied dance and are in your 40s – clearly, you will be unable to pursue this goal as a career. It is not too late, however, to enrol in a ballet class; many ballet schools and local community organizations offer beginner ballet classes for adults. The same applies to many other pursuits that typically must be begun at a relatively early age - in particular, those involving *physical* prowess, be it in dance, athletics, or other forms of physical expression. If you cannot swim, but have always wanted to learn to do so, it is never too late – you should not, however, expect to win a gold medal at the next Olympic Games.

Be positive

This plane of existence that we inhabit is a wondrous and magical place; but it is undeniable that it contains much suffering and unhappiness. We must always be aware of the suffering of others, but also acknowledge that *we are all connected*. This has been said countless times, but it bears repeating – all of us have emerged from the same wellspring, the same source, and we will all, one day, once more rejoin it. Wallowing in despair at the unfairness of this world will not help those who suffer; if children are suffering from poverty or disease, crying in front of our televisions will not help those children (and, in fact, so-called "poverty porn," the disturbing phenomenon of images of horrible suffering and poverty complete with voice-overs begging for charitable donations, does much to belittle and denigrate the victims that it is ostensibly championing, perpetuating the concept of "us" and "them" rather than promoting the truth that we are all in this together). It is only when we ourselves are in a position to help, not only materially, but in other ways – by volunteering, or raising awareness – that we can truly make a difference. If we have led lives that, in retrospect, seem unsatisfying or even unhappy; if we wake up in the morning feeling old or tired; if we sometimes survey our lives, wondering what happened to our once-hopeful selves, full of dreams for a happy and satisfying future; if we dwell on regret over what might have been - we must leave those thoughts aside and turn our attention toward the future, regardless of what our situation is at present. Your future is truly a blank slate, and you are the only one with the power to write on it.

Do not be discouraged by others' negativity

We live in a culture where youth is prized, almost worshipped. Despite the undeniable fact that older adults now see themselves as young and vital for a much longer period than previous generations did, the pursuit of youth (or its appearance, when youth itself is gone) has become almost an obsession for many of us. We will not here lament the fact that youth and inexperience have become more highly prized in modern society than age and experience, which, we are told, were respected and honoured in times past; whether or not this is the case (and it seems to have been, in some societies, at least), dwelling on the loss of centuries-old traditions will not help us achieve our goals. We must look forward, not back! In doing so, however, as we focus on making a real change in our lives, we may find ourselves faced with skepticism from those around us. We may be told that we are too old to make a change that we are being foolish, that we must be going through a mid-life crisis. We must not allow ourselves to be influenced by the negativity that we encounter. Neither must we harbour resentment or anger toward those who may be trying to dissuade us from our new course; they themselves may feel threatened by the changes that they see in us. Think of yourself as a potential inspiration to them!

Be proactive

In the following chapters, we will be looking at the ways in which we can transform our dreams into reality. We will be learning how to aim our focus single-mindedly on the future, disregarding any disappointments or unhappy incidences from our past; we will learn how to tap into the collective unconscious of all living beings on this plane, in order to manifest what we desire. We must not, however, expect that we can simply sit and wait for good things to happen without any work on our part. We have all been told from a very early age that "God helps those who help themselves." This is an undeniable fact, and calls to mind the old joke of the priest who prayed every night to God for a lottery win so that he could use the funds to help the poor among his flock. When months went by without a win, he finally cried out to God, "Why do You ignore me? Why do You not answer my prayer?" – and a voice boomed down from Heaven, "Buy a ticket!"

Know what you want

This may seem obvious, but it is, in fact, far from it. Many of us have vague ideas of how we would like our lives to unfold. We think that we might be happier if we had more money, were younger or better-looking, or had a more interesting partner. We might not, however, be able to point to one or more *specifics*. If we want to pursue change, we must know what we are pursuing change *toward*. We must focus on a goal – or several goals – that we then focus upon unwaveringly. Vague or unformed ideas will not help us achieve anything but a chronic, nagging sense of dissatisfaction. If you are not certain what you want – if all you know is that you do not want what you have – then you must spend some time reading, meditating, or talking with trusted friends or family (who may possess insights that surprise you – you may, for example, have an old friend who clearly remembers what your goals and dreams were years, or even decades, ago). The more specific your goal, the more likely you are to achieve it.

Be yourself

Only you know what your true, deepest desires are. They may be unlike those of your friends, family, or acquaintances. We have all heard of those unfortunate people who have unhappily followed career paths that they were expected to pursue - for example, because their parents were doctors or engineers or police officers, and there was no question of their choosing different careers. While these cases can be extreme (the poet at heart who works as an accountant because it is expected of him), we all, to some degree, often make our choices based on what others expect of us. They may be influenced by our peer group, our teachers, or even the media. What must be understood, however, is that *whatever pursuit is your deepest wish, it is the right one for you* (excluding, of course, anything that brings harm to others). You will never be truly happy if you follow a path that others have laid out for you, but that you feel, in your heart, is wrong for you.

Chapter 8: The Nature of Reality

All of us has, at one time or another, wondered what the meaning of life is. Especially during difficult times, whether the death of a loved one, or the loss of a job or relationship, we may question not only the purpose of our lives, but whether living them is truly worth the trouble.

And what of all the suffering in the world? Everyone has at one time or another wondered at the horrible suffering – both of humans and non-humans – obvious with even a casual glance at the daily news. Children and other innocents are struck down, not only by starvation and war in foreign countries, but by cancers and other diseases, or accidents, here on our doorstep. It seems that if we choose to look for it, we can find suffering everywhere. If we extend our focus to non-humans, a simple visit to any animal shelter – or slaughterhouse - will convince us that no being is immune from suffering. How could a benevolent deity permit such horror?

It is important, first, to acknowledge that what we call reality, which is the world around us as we experience it, filtered through our senses, represents a tiny fraction of what exists. It is instructive to keep several points in mind:

1. Our senses provide us with an arbitrary and limited understanding of the world around us.

Most of us have seen photographs of flowers taken in ultraviolet light meant to simulate the way they are seen by bees and other pollinating insects. Some flowers even have obvious "landing strips," invisible to our own eyes, that guide the insects toward the pollen. This simple example demonstrates in a very concrete way that what we see around us is not necessarily "reality," but one *version* of reality, the one that our eyes have evolved to perceive. As primates, we also tend to rely primarily upon our sense of sight to interpret the world, but there are animals that rely far less on sight and far more on other senses. The dog – a species so closely bound to us, that some believe that it would not have evolved from the wolf at all, if humans did not exist – relies far more on its sense of smell to understand the world. We know that our own scent receptors number approximately five million, whereas the dog's, depending on breed, number in the *hundreds of millions*. We can only imagine, but never truly appreciate, how the dog understands the nature of reality, but we know that it is very different from our own understanding. Can we claim that our understanding is the "true" one? Of course not.

2. What we understand about the universe is dwarfed by what we do not understand.

As twenty-first-century humans living in highly technological societies, we tend to believe that we have unlocked virtually all of the mysteries of the cosmos, and that it is only a matter of time before even the most difficult problems – those of dark energy and dark matter, for example – are solved by science. We look back upon the past, when humans believed that the world was flat, or that the sun revolved around it, with a sense of superiority. In fact, the more that we come to understand the universe around us, the more we realize how much we do not know. One hundred years following the discovery of quantum reality, we still do not understand *why* or *how* quantum mechanics works, we only know that it does; the behavior of subatomic particles is, to us, as bizarre and unsettling today as it was in the early decades of the twentieth century. On the larger scale, dark matter and dark energy remain as inscrutable as ever, despite the time and effort on the part of the most brilliant minds in physics and astronomy to penetrate their mysteries. There are, furthermore, countless theories that attempt to reconcile seemingly irreconcilable features of "reality" as we understand it; most of us have heard of the attempts by physicists to arrive at a "theory of everything" that will explain, in mathematical terms, all of the known forces of nature. These attempts have led to speculation involving multiple universes, extra dimensions, and other theoretical constructs that strike the layperson – and perhaps even the specialist – as bizarre and ultimately unprovable.

3. Paranormal phenomena cannot be completely discounted.

An unfortunate result of our highly scientific and technological twenty-first century society is the growing dichotomy between those "skeptics" – mainly scientists and those who identify as science-minded – who claim that if it cannot be described or quantified scientifically, it does not exist, and those who are open to the possibility of a world beyond that detectable by our senses and our scientific instruments. In fact, though so-called hard proof of paranormal phenomena continues to be elusive, there is much circumstantial evidence pointing to other levels of reality. Near-death experiences, psychic phenomena, visits to seemingly other planes of existence – the list of phenomena that cannot be measured or quantified scientifically is truly endless. We would do well to pay attention to these phenomena. Skeptics are fond of claiming that it is worthwhile to have an open mind, "but not so open that your brains fall out" – however, while we must examine all claims of extrasensory perception or other paranormal phenomena carefully, and certainly not be so credulous that our "brains fall out," neither should we approach such claims with preconceived notions that they are a product of peoples' imaginations or wishful thinking, and nothing more.

4. There is a "collective unconscious" that all human beings share.

A key discovery of the founder of analytical psychology, Carl Jung (whose teachings we will be returning to frequently as we undertake our voyage of self-discovery, self-realization, and fulfilment), the collective unconscious is the repository of shared symbols, or *archetypes*, that we, as members of our species, have access to. Symbols emerging from the collective unconscious frequently "leak into" our dreams, which is why Jung placed such a great emphasis on the significance of dreams. (Freud did, as well, though his approach was quite different, and centred on the *personal* unconscious rather than the collective). This would explain the often-noted similarities in dream images across cultures.

Related to this is the fact, noted among researchers and given prominence in recent times, that when in altered states humans seem to visit very similar alternate dimensions (see, for instance, Graham Hancock's 2005 book, *Supernatural: Meetings with the Ancient Teachers of Mankind*, in which he explores the use of hallucinogens throughout human history to access other dimensions of reality, the *objective* existence of which he believes is evidenced by encounters, across millennia, with *the same beings in the same environments*).

5. Archetypes, or the shared symbols or motifs residing in a species' collective unconscious, provide clues or hints to us as we follow our path to individuation.

The concept of *individuation*, another key component of Jung's teachings, is one of the important steps that we will follow on our path to living the life of our dreams, the life that we *know* that we came here to live (for we did, in fact, *choose* to incarnate in this reality, though we exist behind a veil of forgetfulness, without which we would not strive to reach our greatest potential). In Jungian terms, individuation represents the finding of the self, which occurs as we find the balance between our own, personal unconscious, and the collective unconscious; the self must be in equilibrium with the ego, which is the centre of one's conscious mind, the knowledge that *I am me*, one's sense of self-identity (Jung referred to this as the *ego-self axis*). We will explore the most fruitful ways of restoring this equilibrium, including the archetypal imagery found in our dreams – which dip into the collective unconscious that is constantly streaming below our awareness, but that, in the absence of our conscious awareness which is always engaged in the world around us, can be far more easily accessed when asleep.

6. We can control the path of our lives and create our own reality.

We are the creators of our own reality. We must accept, first, that we have *chosen* to incarnate here, and that the purpose of all of our lives is to experience, learn, and grow as sentient beings. Our lives here on Earth, at this time, are gifts that we have given ourselves. It not only is possible, but imperative, that we live to our fullest potential.

There are four steps that will lead us to the transformation that we desire, when we will finally take control of our futures, and fulfil our destinies:

- Ethical living

- Meditation

- Dream analysis

- Fulfilment

In the following chapters, we will explore, one by one, each step as we begin our journey on the road of transformation and ultimate fulfilment. I hope that you will join me on this exciting journey of discovery!

Part Two

Crafting the Future of Your Dreams

Chapter 9: Ethical Living

There are many dimensions to living an ethical life, which must be our springboard to fulfilling our dreams for a full and satisfying future. If we have followed the advice in Part One, and are trying our best to be compassionate, forgiving, and kind in our present, we are well on the way to crafting the future that we desire. By living ethically, we will bring ourselves into greater alignment with the cosmos, while creating a more just and harmonious reality. We are the creators of our reality; we must use this great power in as just a manner as possible.

What does it mean to live ethically? Ethics teaches us, first and foremost, that we must be aware of others as deserving consideration. There is, of course, vociferous disagreement as to who those "others" might be. For our purposes, we will consider *all sentient* beings – human and nonhuman – as deserving consideration. (This is not the place for a detailed philosophical discussion of animal rights and animal welfare as developed by Peter Singer, Tom Regan, and others; but for those who are interested, there are numerous books and articles on the topic easily accessible on-line).

It is, of course, one thing to agree that all beings deserve our consideration, and that we must live ethically in relation to them; it is quite another both to understand what that means, and to actually engage in ethical living. When faced with the suffering and injustice that we see around us, we may feel overwhelmed with the task at hand; it would do well, then, to approach it in a stepwise fashion.

Step 1: Recognize the suffering of others

It is impossible to attempt to alleviate – or, at the very least, avoid contributing to – the suffering in the world without understanding who is suffering, and in what manner. All of us, even the most generous and kind-hearted, often wear blinkers where the suffering of others is concerned. We may send a donation to an animal welfare organization or to an agency that provides food and other goods for children living in poverty at home or overseas; but we frequently tell ourselves, when face-to-face with this suffering, that we "do not want to think about it."

How many of us bite into a burger, marveling on how juicy or delicious it is, yet give not one thought to the appalling conditions that the cow who provided our meal lived and died in? We wear those same blinkers when consuming eggs or dairy; in fact, we perhaps fool ourselves into believing (erroneously) that animals who provide this type of food do not suffer. Of course, the plight of animals in the factory farming system is not the only suffering that we tend to turn a blind eye to – not because we are cruel, but because we might feel overwhelmed, depressed, or even guilty if we examined it too closely.

For instance, we may be wearing clothing – including items that are very expensive, on trend, or carry a designer label – that was manufactured under near-slavery conditions in factories in the less-developed world. Or, in more general terms, we simply may find ourselves accumulating more and more consumer goods, filling our homes with items that we soon lose interest in, while millions have barely enough to subsist on. We may believe that this consumerism does not result in suffering of people halfway across the world; in fact, there are countless ways in which our societies, driven by often mindless consumption, harm both the planet and its inhabitants.

Step 2: Do what you can to help

Of course, recognizing that others suffer is only the first step; we must also do what we can to help. This might be supporting, financially or through volunteering, organizations that help others. There are countless charities that help the less fortunate, and you may find that you feel somewhat overwhelmed with the number of organizations that solicit funds; you may be uncertain as to which to donate to. There are organizations that rate charities, and you may want to consult their websites. Such organizations are Charity Navigator (in the United States), or Charity Intelligence Canada. Their websites also provide tips on the best way to ensure that your donation gets to those in need.

You may decide to give of your time rather than, or in addition to, your money. Not everyone is in a position to help financially; and though many of us are extremely busy with our jobs and taking care of our families, few of us are unable to spare an hour or two a week to volunteer. Most communities advertise for volunteers, and it should not take more than a few clicks of your mouse to find the website run by your local volunteer organization. Most charities and non-profits rely greatly on volunteers, and are happy for help of all kinds, whether with office work, or more hands-on work. Regardless of your interests and abilities, there is certain to be a volunteer position that is right for you.

If volunteerism is not for you, there are other,

perhaps more subtle ways that you can avoid inadvertently contributing to the misery of others. If you are concerned about the treatment of non-humans in the factory farming system, for example, you may consider changing your eating habits; the best-known proponent of this approach is Gary L. Francione, who promotes veganism as the only ethical option. If, on the other hand, your primary focus is your fellow humans, you might decide to check the label of every garment that you purchase, to be certain, as much as possible, that you are not contributing to the misery of those working under insufferable conditions in factories overseas. As a consumer in the West, your purchasing power can be your greatest weapon in the struggle against injustice.

Step 3: Be fair to the people in your life

Ethical living does not only relate to how you treat strangers or animals; it extends to those nearest and dearest to you, as well as acquaintances and coworkers. This is not always as easy as it seems; in fact, we are often cruelest to those we are closest to. It is instructive to realize that our negative reactions to others can often be explained by *shadow projection*. What does this mean? Jung believed that buried beneath our awareness is a side to our personalities that we keep buried, because it represent a facet of ourselves that we cannot consciously face. Usually, the traits represented by our shadow are negative ones. Of course, as with much of ourselves that is buried beneath our conscious minds, our shadow can manifest in various (typically unpleasant) ways. One is that of its *projection*, where we project our own negative traits onto others. One clue that we are engaging in shadow projection is overreaction. We may find ourselves vehemently arguing with someone over a relatively trivial matter, or reacting strongly and negatively to a real or fictional character on television whom we do not know, but to whom we feel a deep antipathy, for reasons that are unclear to us. We might say, "He gets under my skin," or "She pushes my buttons," not quite knowing why.

If you find yourself overreacting to or becoming very critical of someone, it would be instructive to ask yourself what it is, specifically, about them that you find so irritating or upsetting. Be honest – you may be surprised to discover that what you criticize and abhor in the other, is actually what you abhor in yourself. In fact, this externalizing of what you reject in yourself prevents you from becoming whole, or *balancing of the self and ego*, essential to your process of self-realization.

*

The Problem of Materialism

The issue of materialism is one that all of us who hope to engage in ethical living must face. It is virtually impossible in today's Western developed world to avoid being constantly bombarded with advertisements for the latest material possession, whether clothing, furniture, electronic gadgetry, or any of a myriad of other items that we become convinced are essential for our happiness and wellbeing. We buy lottery tickets, dreaming about what we would purchase with our windfall – huge mansions, designer clothing, or sports cars. We watch reality shows featuring unimaginably wealthy men and women adorned in fabulous clothing and jewelry, seemingly spending all of their time thinking about their appearance, their possessions, or their equally attractive partners. Is it any wonder that we feel dissatisfied with ourselves and our lives, constantly wishing that we had more – more money, more beauty, more youth, more *stuff*?

There is nothing wrong or shameful about wishing for some measure of material comfort, provided that the desire does not develop into obsession or greed. It is also normal to want to look attractive. These are human desires that have existed since the earliest times of our species' evolution; we need only consider the evidence for early humans' having adorned themselves with strings made of shells or ivory beads, dating to many tens of thousands of years ago, to acknowledge that a desire for material possessions, wealth, beauty, or status is hardwired into our DNA. Though many have successfully overcome the desire for material wealth, living simply and with only the basic necessities, it is unrealistic to expect this of the average person living and working in the typical North American city. What we can do, however, is take a hard and realistic look at our materialism, and in this way begin to take a more balanced approach to the consumerism that surrounds us.

Remember: The media's presentation of celebrity is a fantasy

Anyone who remembers what it is like to be a teenager knows that no greater desire exists at that age than that of fitting in. As teenagers, our desire for the "right" clothing or hairstyle feels like a matter of life or death, and we look back on those years with a smile, remembering ruefully how we begged our parents for a certain pair of designer jeans or running shoes. What we must acknowledge is that we are not all that different as adults; though we may be more invested in our individuality, not necessarily wanting to look or behave like everyone else, we express that individuality only within very tight boundaries. We are still striving to be accepted by our peers (or those whom we aspire to emulate), and one way in which we do this is to focus on celebrities – what they are wearing or eating, what brands they promote and where they travel.

What we often forget as we gaze enviously at the perfect faces, bodies, and lifestyles of celebrities is that what we are viewing through the slavering lens of the media is largely artificial. The most obvious example is the ubiquitous use of Photoshop. The images that we see of celebrities on the covers of magazines, on the internet, and even in video or film have been altered to the point where many of them are hardly recognizable. While we gasp at how wonderful a given celebrity looks in her 60s or 70s, what we are viewing is an image where her wrinkles have been digitally erased and her body transformed into that of a 30-year-old. In addition to the distortions presented in photos and video, many celebrities – some of them very young – are using cosmetic surgery and Botox to smooth out wrinkles and worry lines.

One blatant irony surrounding today's celebrity is that, whereas we live in an era where privacy is ostensibly no longer the norm and everyone has become the star of his or her own reality show - posting the most private information and photographs online for all to see - in fact, we know very little about the lives that celebrities are leading. We may think that we know them, but their handlers control much of the information that makes its way to the media. It is surprising that even in an era where paparazzi and television shows or websites trading in salacious gossip are seemingly everywhere, many of us are caught off-guard when a famous couple announces their divorce, having had no idea that there were problems with the marriage.

Remember: Possessions bring no lasting happiness

We heard this from our mothers and from our Sunday school teachers, and perhaps at the time we did not believe them; but since then most of us have discovered the harsh truth that the fulfilment of our desire for this or that possession, while it may provide short-term happiness or even exultation, will quickly lose its lustre. In fact, many of our basements, closets, and attics are full of forgotten items that at one time meant a great deal to us, but that we have not thought about in years.

We may have one or more very special possessions that we would not dream of parting with; this may have been a gift from someone special, or something that we saved up for for years before being able to purchase it and which still gives us pleasure. If we take an honest inventory of all that we own, however, we must admit that very few items have any sentimental value for us at all, and if we were to lose them, we would not miss them.

*

Decluttering and minimalist living

Decluttering and **minimalist living** have become important trends in recent years, as people look around themselves at the mountains of stuff that they own and grow appalled at the number of useless items that they share their lives with. Any one of us can look into our closets and easily pull out countless pieces of clothing that we have not worn in a year or more, and that we will probably never wear, but have not gotten rid of for reasons that can only be called ridiculous – perhaps they will one day once more be in style (and if huge shoulder pads or peasant blouses do come back in style, would you really want to wear them?), or we'll lose that stubborn ten pounds and fit into them again....or perhaps we've simply forgotten that they were hanging in the back of the closet, collecting dust. Most of us have also accumulated knickknacks or other items that sit in boxes or bins, hidden away, perhaps never again to see the light of day, but which we simply cannot bring ourselves to get rid of.

Those who have successfully decluttered their lives, getting rid of excess possessions and resisting the urge to replace them, have found themselves far more content and stress-free than before. They find themselves more able to live within the present – no longer surrounded by possessions that remind them of the past – and spending much less time dusting or cleaning items that are really of very little value to them.

There is no reason to feel overwhelmed by the prospect of completely overhauling your lifestyle. Even getting rid of a little clutter will make you feel remarkably better. Many of us have numerous items that we cannot possibly ever use again. Some of them, like CDs or books, are now available in digital format. How many of us dig through CDs when we want to hear a piece of music, rather than simply playing it on our iPod, smart phone, or other digital medium? Books, too, while possessing charms that admittedly cannot be reproduced by digital readers, take up huge amounts of room. If you love your books and cannot imagine parting with them – look through them. Are you certain that you will one day want to pull out and re-read every single one? You can use the same logic while going through the clothing in your closet, or the dishes, glasses, pots, and pans in your kitchen.

If we think of how simply our ancestors lived, or of how many disadvantaged people there are living very simple lives in the world today, it is almost embarrassing to consider the sheer volume of unnecessary items cluttering up our lives. It is also instructive to realize that many of the things that we don't use or need can be of use to someone else. In recycling such items by giving them away, we are helping others – and the planet – while helping ourselves.

*

Again, it is important to stress that there is nothing evil, unethical, or morally wrong about desiring material wealth or abundance. What is important is to maintain a balanced view of material possessions, and to avoid becoming obsessed with accumulating more and more money, more and more *things*.

The Dalai Lama has pointed out that he has met some of the world's wealthiest people – millionaires and billionaires several times over – and many of them are very unhappy. If we are struggling to put food on the table or keep a roof over our heads, this may seem incredible to us, but it is a truism that material wealth is no guarantee of happiness. Otherwise, we would not have so many cases of the extremely wealthy becoming addicted to drugs or alcohol, or committing suicide.

Finally, as we strive to live ethically, there are a few points that we should keep in mind:

Financial issues are one of the most common causes of stress in modern lift

It is true that there will always be the poor among us, who struggle on a daily basis to feed themselves and their families; but financial stress is also a common factor in the lives of middle class and even upper class people. Why is this so? Of course, living beyond our means is the most common reason, and this can be traced to the mindless consumerism that is driving our desire to want more and more. If we make a concerted effort to live within our means, we can reduce much of the stress of our daily lives.

We aren't going to live forever

One of the most famous teachings of the Buddha was that all is transitory, and it is, in fact, this lack of permanence that leads to our dissatisfaction. It is the reason that many of our spiritual teachers emphasize the importance of living in the moment – not dwelling on the past or dreaming of the future. Though there is no reason to wallow in depression over the fact of our eventual and inescapable deaths, the fact remains that we will, in fact, die one day, and we will be leaving behind all of these material goods that we thought were so essential to our happiness. Will they seem so critically important to us when we are old, perhaps ill, and on our deathbeds? That is very unlikely. In fact, though there are many regrets voiced by the dying – such as they wished they had been less cautious, or had said "I love you" more often – none we have heard of have expressed regret that they did not accumulate more material possessions.

Imagine that you died today –imagine leaving your loved ones with the task of having to go through your possessions, deciding what to keep, what to dispose of, or what to give away. Look around yourself at all that you have, and ask yourself whether you would feel proud, or embarrassed, to leave your loved ones with the task of sorting through it all.

Someone less fortunate may make use of your rarely-used possessions.

Though most of us would not consider ourselves hoarders, many of us do have rarely- or never-used items cluttering up our closets, cupboards, and spare rooms. We may feel reluctant to part with them – claiming sentimental value, or that we may, one day, find a need for them – but in fact, we hardly think of these items unless our attention is drawn to them. We do not need them, but some less fortunate person may. Every city has organization that collect donations of money and goods for the less fortunate; consider giving away possessions that you rarely or never use. You will breathe more freely in your less-cluttered environment, and you will be helping others, as well.

*

As we work toward living an ethical life, moving away from the self-centred focus that we are encouraged to maintain by the consumerism and superficiality that confronts us daily, we make a space for good things to flow into our lives. This is a core principle of *feng shui* – the ancient Chinese belief system that encourages positive energy flow by harmonizing one's environment according to certain rules.

If your mind and your surroundings are both cluttered by negative or unnecessary thoughts or objects, respectively, you will block any possibility of achieving harmony with your environment, immediate and cosmic. Once you begin working on ethical living, you will find that, without even trying, you will begin to draw positive forces to you.

Let us now move on to the next step in our journey toward a fulfilling life – meditation.

Chapter 10: Meditation

There is no better way to connect with your higher self than through meditation. Your higher self is your true self – called the soul by some – which emanates from, and is part of, the Source. It is difficult to maintain a close connection with our higher selves, given how enmeshed we are in this physical world, but it is essential to do so if we hope to live to our fullest potential.

There are countless benefits to meditation, and virtually no drawbacks. Though our focus here is on the psychological and spiritual benefits of the practice, meditation also can have positive effects on overall stress levels, which can potentially lead to improved physical health.

There are as many ways to meditate as there are meditators. Some are firmly grounded in religious practice – Hindu, Buddhist, Christian, and so on, whereas more recently, especially in the West, there has been a trend toward non-religious meditation, such as mindfulness meditation in its various forms. Despite what some of these traditions might insist, there is absolutely no "right" way to meditate, and you are welcome to take something from one tradition and something from another, or even create your own form of meditation, if you wish. Nonetheless, there are some basic guidelines that it makes sense to follow, if you hope to be a successful meditator.

Time and place

It is important that you choose a time and place to meditate that is relatively free of distractions; a television blaring in the background, or an area of the house where children are playing, are not conducive to success. Some meditators prefer the early morning, before the rest of the household has awoken; others may find that they are too groggy at this time, and likely to fall asleep where they sit. Others meditate before bed. Choose a time and place that is likely to present you with no interruptions for as long as you intend to sit, whether ten minutes or an hour.

Posture

Posture in meditation is a means to an end – that of bringing your physical self as close as possible to harmony with the Source, and with the universe. This is impossible if you are feeling uncomfortable, cramped, or in pain. There is no hard and fast rule with regard to posture; in fact, there are types of meditation, such as walking meditation, where the body is not even kept still. It is also certainly acceptable to lie down or sit on a chair (though lying down has the disadvantage of sometimes leading to drowsiness and sleep). What is important with regard to posture is that you be able to breathe deeply and comfortably, and encourage a stillness within. Typically, the posture taken while meditating is that of sitting cross-legged with as naturally straight a spine as possible, so that an imaginary straight line leads from the base of the spine to the sky. Sitting on a special cushion is, of course, not necessary, but can be helpful, in that proper sitting slightly tilts the pelvis, placing the spine in an ideal position of alignment. You can keep your eyes open or closed, whichever is most comfortable; Zen meditators sit facing the wall with eyes open, though in other traditions, the eyes are kept closed.

Breathing

The breath is central to meditating successfully. Indeed, "following the breath," where the focus is placed on one's breathing, is central to many traditions. Whether or not you choose to focus on your breath when meditating, what is necessary is that you be able to breathe evenly, deeply, and freely. If your posture, or your clothing, is such that you feel your breathing restricted, you must adjust it.

You may choose to count your breaths, or to simply be aware of your breathing as a way to focus your mind while meditating. This is a technique used in many traditions (including that of Vipassana, a Buddhist form of meditation). You may focus on the place where your breath enters your nose, being lightly aware of your breathing in and out; or, conversely, you may focus on your diaphragm and the rising and falling of your belly. You may count your breaths, perhaps to 10 and then back down to 1. Whatever is the most comfortable and natural to you, is the technique that you should use.

What about using a **mantra**? This is a technique where a word or phrase – in popular culture, typically "*Om*," though of course it can be any appropriate word, series of words, or sound – is repeated to oneself as a way of focusing the mind. According to those practitioners who use mantras to meditate, the advantages can be many; some believe that the universe has a *sound*, and that the proper mantra can bring the meditator into harmony with the frequency of that sound.

Focus

In most forms of meditation, it is important to *focus the mind*. The way that you choose to do this

– whether by counting breaths or chanting a mantra, or even playing a recording of ocean waves or other sounds – is entirely up to you (despite what the various traditions may insist upon). By learning to focus your mind – that is, working to discipline your mind so that it does not flit from one thought to another – you will find a peace and calm that you could not hope to experience while rushing about your day.

Pay attention to images, thoughts, and memories that come up

While you do not want to spend your time thinking about what you are going to do today, or what you did yesterday, once you have gained some experience in quietening your mind, you will find that unbidden thoughts, memories, and images will flow into your consciousness. Some may be very pleasant, but others may not be. Pay attention to these – they are messages from your personal unconscious, as well as from the collective unconsciousness, which is how the Source communicates with us at the level below our conscious awareness. If you pay attention to the messages that you receive when your mind is quiet, you can find clues to the true meaning of your existence, and the tasks - and education - that you chose to incarnate here to undertake.

*

How long should you spend meditating, and how often? That is truly up to you, though it is more important to meditate often, than it is to meditate for a long time. If you can only manage ten minutes a day at the outset, that is fine, so long as you do it regularly (preferably daily). Most people find that they cannot sit still and focus their minds for more than five or ten minutes when they first begin meditating, though they find that within a few weeks, they have extended their sessions to twenty minutes or half an hour, without really trying. They also find that their thoughts, while very scattered and difficult to control at the outset, soon become quietened. At first, it may be difficult to keep your mind focused for more than a few seconds at a time, though you will find, with practice, that your mind will become disciplined rather quickly.

You may wish to experiment with various ways of meditating – with eyes open, eyes closed, with a mantra or without – and various postures, until you find the one, or ones, that you are most comfortable with. It is not important that you follow a specific set of rules; what is important is that you find a practice that is right for you.

As you become more practiced and experienced

with meditating, and as your mind begins to quieten, you will find that thoughts and images begin to seep into your conscious mind. They may seem unusual, or even incomprehensible. Do not dismiss them, especially if you find that the same images and thoughts are visiting you again and again. These are messages that you must pay attention to, as the universal wisdom is communicating to you and drawing your attention to what is important for you, if you wish to live as you were meant to.

These messages will likely represent *archetypes*, those universal symbols that provide meaning to all human beings. (Some common archetypes are, for example, those of the mother, the wise old woman, the hero – symbols that have been fraught with meaning throughout human history, and within all cultures). They are, in one sense, a version of Plato's *forms* - ideal representations, existing in a perfect realm beyond our grasp, of all that exists in our imperfect world. We do not expect to encounter, in our day-to-day lives, *perfect* representations of these archetypes, which reside as ideas or symbols only, in the collective unconscious.

Be certain to recognize any hint of shadow projection

Not all thoughts or images that emerge while you are meditating will be comforting or positive ones. You may, in fact, find yourself dwelling on a real or imagined insult, or on a past event, that you find upsets or even angers you. Perhaps a long-forgotten incident – an argument you had with a friend, or a perceived snub – suddenly floods your memory. Ask yourself what the meaning is. What is the universe trying to tell you? Ask yourself whether this is your shadow expressing itself. Is the message that you need to recognize some unpleasant trait in yourself – something that you must do, if you hope to address it, and work on it?

If you find yourself subject to a recurring thought or image, write it down. Take a few minutes, once you have finished meditating, to sit quietly and analyze the image. Can it represent an archetypal symbol – that of friend, mother, hero? The list of archetypes is a huge one, perhaps even endless, but you should be able to recognize the archetype, or symbol, represented. For instance, say the image of an animal – a wolf – begins to present itself to you. You have never seen a wolf except in photos or film, and have never spent much time thinking about wolves, yet here you are, sitting and meditating, minding your own business, and the image of a wolf begins to intrude upon your calm. Clearly, this is a message that you must pay attention to. Ask yourself what it might represent. Wolves have existed alongside humans for at least many tens of thousands of years; were it not for wolves living in proximity to early humans, we would almost certainly not have our domestic dog. The wolf has certainly impressed itself upon the human psyche in a way that most other animals have not. It is smart, pitiless, single-minded, strong, and lethal. Is your higher self trying sending you a message that you need to be more forceful, to go after what you want? Have you been too mild-mannered – too sheep-like – in your career or in your personal life? On the other hand, it could be that you have been behaving *too* aggressively, running roughshod over others' feelings and interests. You may choose to engage in psychotherapy or analysis with a professional, but *you* are the best person to interpret the meaning of the symbols that come to you when your mind is open to them.

Meditation is a vital and valuable step on your journey toward self-realization and the crafting of the life you desire. There is, however, more work to do. Once you have practiced living ethically to free yourself of clutter, self-centredness, and excessive materialism, and you are coming close to achieving the calm, receptive state that necessarily comes with regular meditation, you will be ready explore your dreams.

Chapter 11: Dream Analysis

There is much controversy surrounding our dreams, and whether they have any meaning at all. Some argue that dreams are simply the random firings of our neurons, and ultimately meaningless; others believe that dreams are made up of stitched-together experiences, given something of a narrative structure by our subconscious minds; yet others believe that dreams can predict the future, resolve past conflicts, or provide vital clues to help us our in our waking lives.

In fact, dreams are fraught with meaning. When asleep, our unconscious mind dips into the continually flowing stream of the collective unconscious, sending to us images and symbols originating in both that great repository and in our own, personal unconscious. These are messages from our higher selves and from the Source. If we struggle to understand what our purpose for being is, we would do well to pay close attention to our dreams.

If you are someone who rarely remembers your dreams, or who wakes up with a memory that quickly fades, so that you say to yourself, "I know that I had an interesting dream, but I just can't quite put my finger on it" – an experience that we all have sometimes – then the best solution is to keep a pencil and paper (or tablet) by your bedside, so that you can record your dream as soon as you awaken with the memory of it fresh in your mind.

Dreams come to us in a variety of forms. Some are simply disjointed vignettes, disconnected scenes or images that follow each other, seemingly without any logical order. Others may be complex stories with plots and subplots, involving multiple people, perhaps from our past or present, or perhaps unknown to us in waking life. Some people have recurring dreams (or nightmares); sometimes these recurring dreams advance the "plot" more and more each time they are dreamt. Some dreams are vivid; others may seem, upon awakening, to fade into nothingness like a puff of smoke. All dreams, however, contain within them messages that we can choose to heed, or not.

If you have been meditating consistently, allowing images and impressions to flow unresisted into your conscious mind, once you begin paying attention to your dreams you will find that the same symbols, images, and thoughts occur in your dreams; there will be a synchronicity between the two. This is a sign that you are receiving messages about your purpose in life, and whether you are on the right path.

Don't be discouraged if at first you have difficulty remembering your dreams, even with pencil and paper on your night table, or if the images and sequences that you do remember seem to make no sense; it does take practice to remember, and to recognize, the messages coming to you while you are asleep.

You spend approximately one-third of your life asleep (if you don't, you should!) and, according to experts, roughly two hours dreaming every night. Sleep is restorative and regenerative; without sufficient sleep, most of us cannot function at our full capacity. Given that we spend so much time in the alternate reality (and it is a reality) of our dreams, it is surprising, even shocking, that most of us pay so little attention to it. Exploration of this little-known realm can only lead to clarity and enlightenment.

Taking notice of symbols in our dreams

Not every symbol or theme that appears in our dreams is of significance. In fact, we often simply relive incidents that occurred the previous day, or, if we are feeling stressed or depressed, we may have a nightmare featuring one of our phobias – spiders, or heights. What helps us to recognize a meaningful symbol or theme that requires our attention and analysis is its *repetition* (though it may not always reappear in the same form), as well as our *reaction* to it.

Repetition

To return to the example above, if you find yourself often dreaming about wolves (especially if you have never particularly thought about, or been around, wolves), the universe is clearly sending you a message. Be aware, however, that, as a symbol of something deeper, the archetype represented by the wolf in your dreams, can and most likely will also appear in a different form, and this in itself is a clue to the archetype's relevance to your own life. If you have repressed sexual urges that you find difficult to acknowledge – which is certainly one plausible interpretation of the wolf archetype – they may be represented in your dreams not only by wolves, but also by snakes, for example.

Reaction

A strong reaction to an image or symbol in our dreams – in particular what would seem to be an overreaction – is a clue to its significance. We have already touched on overreaction when discussing *shadow projection* – the projection onto others of a negative characteristic that we unconsciously acknowledge in ourselves. Strong reactions to seemingly innocuous phenomena are always a good indication that we need to pay attention to the triggers.

Interpreting the Messages That We Are Given

It will do us little good to recognize the messages being sent to us, if we are unable to read them. It is important to realize that these messages are *meant* to be understood, and with a little effort, we can easily make sense of them. It stands to reason that the universe – represented by our higher selves - would not communicate with us in a way that we could not possibly understand.

Though there are resources to avail ourselves of in the interpretation of our dream and meditative imagery, including countless books and professionals who engage in dream analysis, we are more than equipped to analyze these images ourselves. To that end, we will here examine a few key concepts that Jung developed in his quest to explore our dreams and their significance. (Though he focused on dreams, certainly we must consider the images and symbols that come to us while meditating as equally significant to those that come to us in our dream state. The two are linked).

It is important to remember that it is never too

late to engage in this process. Whether you are 20, 30, or 80, so long as you are alive, you can engage the process of fulfilling your purpose.

Jung believed that our dreams provided us with valuable insights. He coined the term "amplification" in dream analysis to refer to the process of expanding upon the imagery in the dream – drilling down to uncover the layers of meaning and associations within a symbol or image. In this way, Jung believed that we could discover hidden truths about ourselves. In fact, we go further than Jung, believing that these insights are in fact messages from our higher selves, transmitted via symbols residing in the collective unconscious that links all humans (all beings are connected via their collective unconscious, including nonhuman animals). If we pay close attention to these messages, we will be well on the way to self-realization and thus to fulfilling our destinies.

Let us look at an example of a dream, and try to uncover its hidden messages:

You are your much-younger self – perhaps eight or ten years old – and you are skipping through a flower-filled garden. It is springtime; a gentle breeze is blowing through the trees, and birds are chirping all around you. It is nothing like the back yard you played in when you were a child, though you know, in the dream, that this is your back yard. Suddenly, a bird swoops down to peck at you, and then flies away, up, up, over the fence, and away. You chase it, jumping up and grabbing at it, though of course it is out of your reach. Still, you jump up as you run, trying your best to catch the bird. You watch helplessly as it flies up into the sky and out of view.

Can you find the messages in this dream? There are many, all open to interpretation. Your task would be to interpret its meaning as it applies to you. The universe will not send you messages that you cannot understand, or that you are likely to interpret incorrectly.

For instance, in our example above, the bird clearly represents a key concept. Birds are often viewed as representing freedom, renewal, or transformation. The bird pecking at you and then flying off could be the universe tapping you on the shoulder, as if to say – listen! Maybe you have been plodding along, in a rut, not really aware that the days are going by while you continue on in a job, or in a relationship, that is hindering you in fulfilment of your full potential. The garden may represent a fantasy world of sorts that you have been living in – you are living as though you still have your entire life ahead of you to accomplish what you are meant to, when in fact you need to be jarred out of your complacency and shown that time is not standing still – you must begin to make a change *now*. Alternately, the message may be intended to remind you of how, as a child, all possibilities were open to you; the world was your garden and you could take any path that you chose; yet you are still, in a way, that child, in that it is never too late to change your life.

Remember that interpreting your dreams and the symbols and messages that are sent to you should not feel like a chore; it should be a joyful exercise, as on this voyage of discovery you uncover much about yourself and your purpose in life that you had been unaware of up to now. It doesn't matter whether you're in your 20s, 50s, 70s, or whether you're unemployed, in a dead-end job, or in a satisfying career; it is never too late for anyone to make positive changes in his or her life. All we need do is pay attention to what is being revealed to us.

Intuition

We have all experienced "hunches," which are a form of intuitive knowledge. Some of us have learned to rely upon our intuition more than others; but all of us have access to this rich source of knowledge. As we grow more comfortable in our meditative practice and in our dream work, we deepen our connection with our higher selves, and will become natural for our intuition begins to play a larger role in our everyday lives.

We need to follow our hunches, listen to our intuition, without fearing that we are only imagining what we desire (which is one way in which we talk ourselves out of following the path that we were meant for). It is natural to be fearful of change, especially if we have grown comfortable in our somewhat unsatisfying, yet safe and predictable, lives.

Lucid dreaming

One way in which you can encourage archetypal imagery in your dreams is through *lucid dreaming*. This is a technique that seems to come naturally to some, and, unfortunately, seems out of reach for others. Proponents of lucid dreaming, however, insist that it can be learned. What is lucid dreaming? It is the ability to influence or direct the course of one's dream, all the while *knowing* that one is dreaming. (The term "lucid" refers to the understanding, on the part of the dreamer, that he or she is, in fact, in a dream).

There are those who insist that anyone can learn to lucid dream. Most techniques rely upon the dreamer telling herself or himself, as s/he drifts off to sleep – "I will remember my dream, and I will recognize that I am dreaming." Repeating this assertion night after night will eventually result in a lucid dream. *Dream recall*, as discussed above, is the first step to dreaming lucidly; as you become accustomed to recording your dreams immediately upon awakening, you will eventually find that you can remember them for a longer and longer period of time. Another frequently-suggested technique involves asking oneself frequently throughout the day, *while awake* – "Am I dreaming?" You can do a *reality check*, looking at something, such as a watch, then looking away and looking back to see whether the numbers changed or look strange. Are you dreaming, or are you awake? (This is one recommendation for beginners from Lucidity Institute, an organization that trains people to dream lucidly).

Lucid dreaming is an ideal way to engage our higher selves in conversation; to literally ask questions of the universe, and receive the answers that we seek. One fruitful technique is to focus your mind as you drift off to sleep, telling yourself – and the universe – that you wish to remain aware that you are dreaming, and retain the ability to influence your dream. It is helpful to devise a scenario, making it as detailed as possible. You may, for example, envisage yourself sitting in a café, face-to-face with your higher self (imagine what this entity might look like – it may be you, or an animal, or someone you have never met), having a conversation. You can imagine yourself asking questions – for example, "What is my true purpose?" "Why did I choose to incarnate in this body, at this time?" "What lessons am I here to learn?" As you drift off to sleep, hold these thoughts in your mind. Don't give up – lucid dreaming is not a technique (for it is a technique) that you can learn in a few nights. It does take perseverance and practice. The rewards, however, are more than worth the work.

Be alert to coincidences and synchronicities

One of the most powerful ways in which the universe communicates with us is through the use of apparent coincidences. You may have been following the suggestions outlined in this volume, and have reached the conclusion that you should have followed your dream of being an artist; however, you may feel overwhelmed and discouraged by the task at hand for a number of reasons (self-doubt, for example, or finances) and wonder whether you are simply engaging in wishful thinking. Suddenly, you start to notice a number of coincidences. You attend a party where you are immediately drawn to someone whom you then discover has the same last name as your favourite artist; you receive unsolicited mail advertising courses at an art school in your neighbourhood; while searching for something in the attic, you instead find drawings that you had made in younger years, and that you had forgotten you possessed. Each one of these incidents could individually be considered mere coincidence; but as these "coincidences" accumulate, you must acknowledge that the message to you is loud and clear: *follow your dream!* It is why you incarnated here, and it is the path, not only to your own fulfillment, but to your helping others. We are here, after all, not to satisfy our own selfish needs, but to learn to love and respect others.

Focus

By this point in your journey, you should be ready to focus on your goal with single-minded understanding. You have been given clear indications of what your life's purpose is, and though it may seem difficult, if not impossible, to get from here to there, the universe will make your path, if not easy, then clear and feasible. We often have to work for what we desire, which makes the achievement all the more sweet. Though we may now have a clear vision of what our lives should look like, we still must be prepared to work to achieve our goals.

In the next chapter, we will look at the final step in our transformation – that of fulfilment.

Chapter 12: Fulfilment

You have incarnated here, at this time, to fulfil a plan. The ultimate goal is to learn. Those who have passed over to the other side and have returned – whether as a result of near death experiences, or hypnosis, or mediumship work – almost always report that the true purpose of our existence is to love. It may take many incarnations for a soul to finally live through love, and so we must see each life as a stepping stone on the journey toward ultimate enlightenment.

Though much evil is done in the world, even those who do the most evil are here to learn. Those who have investigated that place where our souls reside between lifetimes tell us that we choose the issue that we must work on in our next incarnation, and in some cases, souls may agree to interact in specific ways when they next incarnate. One soul may agree to be victimized by the other, for instance, especially if that soul was the aggressor in a past life. This is one way in which the concept of *karma*, that "what goes around comes around," works through reincarnation.

If we are honest with ourselves, turning an

analytical eye inward, we will probably be able to pinpoint those behaviors or thoughts that prevent us from living through love. No one is free of negative traits, and most of us, if honest, can identify those that we are most prone to. It might be pride, or self-pity, or a tendency to criticize others. Rather than feeling self-disgust or helplessness, we should look upon these unpleasant traits in ourselves as hurdles to overcome, and lessons to learn. Each soul seems to have certain challenges, and with each incarnation the intention is to work on one or more of these. Pride, for example, might be a challenge for a given soul; that soul will keep incarnating until it learns the harm that this trait does to itself and to others. It is not unusual to see the same pattern of thinking or behavior in one lifetime after the next, when undergoing reincarnation. Until a given lesson is learned, the same challenges, though in different guises, will keep presenting, lifetime after lifetime.

The key to learning through incarnation is *free will*. Though we have chosen the life we are born into before our birth, the way we live this life is not scripted. We have a purpose and an aim, but we can easily steer ourselves off course. This typically happens because we are not overcoming one of the traits that we have come here to work on. Perhaps we tend to be self-centred, obsessively worrying about how others perceive us; this may prevent us from fulfilling a purpose to look outward more rather than always inward, and help others by undertaking a line of work that is not financially rewarding, but is ultimately fulfilling. We may, instead, find ourselves climbing the corporate ladder, achieving one success after the next and garnering the admiration of those around us, but feeling unfulfilled or even depressed. The lesson that we were meant to learn, that focussing on the needs of others is more important than obsessing over our own selfish desires, has been ignored. If we do not learn this lesson in *this* lifetime, we will surely find ourselves in a future lifetime faced with the same type of choice.

Hopefully, at this point in our journey of self-realization, we have a good idea of what our lives should look like, though we may be uncertain how to get from here to there. The good news is – the hard part is over! Most people who are unhappy or feel dissatisfied know that they want their lives to be different, but have no idea how they want them to be different. People may say, "I wish I had a different job," or "I wish I had more money," or even, "I wish I could win the lottery" – but if pressed, cannot articulate a detailed picture of what their day-to-day lives would be like if they had what they wish for. A vague wish for more money, or even for fabulous wealth, is not a plan. In fact, study after study has shown that the category of people among those we tend to envy the most – lottery winners – are jubilant when they win, but over time, they return to their baseline: if they were depressed or unsatisfied or unfulfilled beforehand, they eventually return to feeling the same way once the excitement of their windfall fades. Remember – money cannot buy happiness. It may be true that financial struggle can lead to stress or even depression, but if money were the key to happiness or fulfilment, we would not see so much obvious misery among celebrities and others who never need worry about money.

Humans are social animals. We do not live in a vacuum; we are embedded in society. Even the most antisocial among us still need to interact with others, whether it be in person with the cashier at the grocery store, on the telephone with the utility company, or online. Very few people are completely self-sufficient, living in complete isolation. In fact, it is virtually impossible to life in that way in today's world. Some thinkers believe that human consciousness – our subjective feeling of being an "I" – can only develop in relation to others. In otherwords, consciousness as we understand it would not exist for someone born and raised in total isolation, without contact with other humans (a virtual impossibility, of course, though there have been a few celebrated cases of children apparently raised by animals, with no contact with other humans, and only found many years later; it is difficult to evaluate these children's internal experience, as none of them could use language and had great difficulty acquiring it. Of course, animals are also beings, thus it may be that contact with *any* being, whether human or not, will lead to the development of self-awareness, or consciousness).

Given the fact that we all exist within a web of humanity, and that few people, if any, could survive and thrive in isolation, we must acknowledge that the wellbeing of our fellow humans must be as important to us as our own. Our survival depends on others, and what improves the quality of life of those around us improves our own. If we focus on enriching ourselves at the expense of others, or of hoarding material goods whether or not we need them when others could benefit from them, we are ignoring the most important lesson that we are here to explore – that of loving others – and we cannot expect to achieve a life that is meaningful and fulfilling.

Four Steps To Self-Actualization

1. Visualization
2. Consistency
3. Persistence
4. Optimism

1. Visualization

At this point in your journey, you know what your life should look like. Feel free to fantasize, imagining yourself living as you were meant to. You can, if you like, hold these images in your mind as you drift off to sleep or ride to your workplace every day, or whenever you have free time – it is, in fact, not at all an idle use of free time, but a constructive one.

Use visualization while meditating. Create an image in your mind of what you desire; this could be an image of yourself engaging in the activity that you have come to realize is your purpose in this life. Hold that image, meditating upon it, pulling your mind back to it whenever you become distracted. You can tie it to a mantra, or to your breath. It is very important that you focus upon it, not as a wish, but as *reality*. The more you meditate upon this image, the more you internalize it and make it who you are, right now.

You may feel awkward or embarrassed, or even ridiculous, when you first begin to use visualization, especially if you have never been prone to fantasy or speculation; but the more you do so, the easier it will become. Soon you will be so comfortable with visualization that whenever you have an idle moment, you will find the image or series of images that you use coming into your conscious experience. You will also begin to *believe* it as reality. You may find that for a few seconds – or perhaps even minutes – you had forgotten that this new life had not yet manifested; you had been thinking and feeling as though it in fact had.

Put the time before you drift off to sleep to good use; this can be a fruitful time to create even an elaborate scenario, imagining "a day in the life" of the new you. Imagine yourself engaging in conversation with the people around you – your family, your friends or co-workers. Make these images or sequences as detailed as possible. You can think of them as scenes from your life, sent to you from the future. This can be your "alternate life," the place you visit in your mind, the place where the *real* you resides. Of course, it isn't recommended that you "check out" while driving or operating heavy machinery! But you should think of these interludes as representing reality.

It is obvious that if you do not truly *believe* that

you are capable of success, you cannot succeed. As you become more experienced with visualization, your success – whatever that represents – will seem not only easily attainable, but just around the corner. In fact, the more that you see yourself as the new you, the more that you visualize yourself as the new you *in the present*, the more you will *become* the new you.

2. Consistency

You are sending messages out to the universe, signaling that you are ready to become what you were always intended to be. Be certain to be consistent, both in the messages that you are sending and in those that you are internalizing. Confusing, mixed, or sporadic messages will only lead to disappointment. It will not help to use the visualization described in the section above if you engage in it only occasionally, allowing your mind to drift to other, less relevant issues as you meditate or drift off to sleep. You must have a laser-like focus, and use that focus to engage in visualization as frequently as possible – at least once a day, preferably more often. Some people place photos representing their desires in prominent areas – on their computer desktops or cell phones, or even taped to the refrigerator – so that they can be reminded frequently throughout the day to work on their visualization.

3. Persistence

Consistency is pointless without persistence. We must remember that patience is of the utmost importance when making a request of the universe; impatience and easy frustration will get us nowhere. Even when we feel that our desires will never be fulfilled, finding ourselves tempted to give up, we must persist. The universe is billions of years old, and will continue to exist billions – if not trillions – of years into the future. Our lives on Earth are but a flicker in that virtual eternity.

It is an unfortunate truth that today, as inhabitants of modern societies, we expect virtually instant gratification of any need or desire that we may have. If we do not get what we want *immediately*, we are disappointed, or even angry. This is a by-product of living as a member of what was once known as the "MTV generation," that generation raised on video clips that were expected to tell a story in two minutes or so; any longer, and the watchers' attention drifted. This tendency has, of course, become exacerbated with the easy availability of all forms of entertainment at our fingertips, whether on our cell phones, computers, or televisions. If we need to know something, we can find the information almost instantly. It is astonishing to realize that in our parents' and grandparents' days, information was much less readily available – and, more importantly, one had to work to get it, perhaps by taking a trip to the library or looking it up in an encyclopedia. We cannot imagine having to wait so long to satisfy our desire to know something. We expect our needs and desires to be almost instantly gratified. This, of course, applies by extension not only to information, but to any need or desire that we may have.

The universe does not follow the breathless, second-to-second pace of our lives. An entire lifetime is but a blip in the life of the universe; it is, in fact, a blip in our own lives, when viewed along the trajectory of their entirety, comprising all of our lives, past, present, and future. As such, we have to understand that our requests are unlikely to be responded to as quickly as we would like. We have been heard; we simply must be patient for the response. It is important, in this reality, to maintain consistency, persistence, and focus, so that the requests that we send to the universe do not break down or become unclear.

4. Optimism

It is easy to become depressed and out of sorts when our desires are not met immediately. We must remember that a positive attitude attracts positive people and things into our lives. Of course, sometimes bad things happen; if they did not, there would be no point to our existence, as we would learn nothing. We have incarnated here, after all, to learn and grow. Learning through the bad times give us a greater appreciation for the good in our lives.

Except for those unfortunate people among us who suffer from clinical depression or similar mental illnesses – and most of these can be treated very effectively with medication, psychotherapy, or a combination of the two – we all choose how to view the world, through a glass half-empty or half-full. Optimism *is* a choice.

For those of us who find it difficult to remain optimistic and positive, and who find ourselves falling into a familiar pattern of pessimism, negativity, and even hopelessness, there are strategies that we can use to brighten our outlook and increase our optimism.

First, we have to ask ourselves what we gain by being pessimistic. We may dislike admitting this, but if we hold onto negative feelings, we *must* be gaining something from them. It may be that others shower us with attention, commiserating with us and thus rewarding us for our self-pity, or trying to convince us that life isn't that terrible, after all. It may be that by drawing negative energy to ourselves, we continually reinforce our beliefs that nothing good can happen to us, and be gaining a measure of self-satisfaction because we are repeatedly being proved right. We may immerse ourselves in all the bad news on television and online, and tell ourselves that only someone naïve or unintelligent can possibly remain positive when faced with such a constant barrage of crises and negative events; thus, we tell ourselves, we must be particularly perceptive and intelligent. It is a useful exercise to ask yourself what you are gaining by your negativity. Be honest; it may surprise you to admit to yourself that you are, in fact, benefiting from maintaining a pessimistic worldview.

Once you have honestly decided to cultivate a more positive attitude, there are several exercises that you can engage in. Some may seem incredibly simple, but they are also incredibly effective.

Smile

This advice may sound almost insultingly simple, but smiling is, in fact, one of the best ways to lift your mood. Research has shown that even a forced, artificial smile will lead to benefits of mood – and, incidentally, of health, with an increase in beneficial hormones and neurotransmitters. The more you force yourself to smile, the more you will smile naturally. Soon, it will become second nature, and you will find that you now face life not only with a smile, but with a much more optimistic outlook.

Make a list of all your blessings

How often we forget how fortunate we truly are! It is a useful exercise to take pen and paper – or sit at your tablet or computer – and compile a list of all that is positive in your life. You may have children, a loving partner, a beautiful home, or less tangible blessings – good health, or a love of reading. Have you ever had an accident or illness and been hospitalized? Most of us have at least had some medical intervention, even one as simple as a course of antibiotics for a minor infection. Ask yourself whether you would have been so easily cured, had you lived a century ago instead of today. Have you had appendicitis, or cataracts? You could easily have died of one and been blinded by the other, had you not been living in the twenty-first century. Rather than wallow in our self-pity or pessimism, we should take a step backward and look at our lives from the perspective of human history. The humans who emerged in Africa two hundred thousand years ago were physically no different from us. Imagine what the life of an average human then must have been like. What about the life of a human living one thousand years ago? Or even one hundred years ago? Do we really have anything to complain about?

Expose yourself to positive influences

This has been said before, but it cannot be said too often. Use your judgment when deciding what to read, or what to watch on television or online.

Don't overindulge in mind-altering substances

It is an unfortunate truth that while under the influence of drugs or alcohol, we may feel quite happy and positive – but there will be an inevitable hangover, where we may feel physically ill and spiritually depleted. Especially if we tend to have a negative outlook, moderation is essential when consuming these substances. Ideally, we should not consume them at all.

Conclusion: The Life You've Always Dreamed Of

It is inevitable that if you follow the guidelines laid before you in this book, you will find yourself, at this point in your journey, not only living a much more rewarding and satisfying life, but living with an understanding of why you are here, and how you should continue living as your future unfolds.

You incarnated here to fulfil a purpose. Part of what makes being human rewarding is that we have free will; we are here to learn and to grow, but we are not forced to go in any one direction. We can choose to pursue our true purpose, or not; it is up to us alone. We must always remember compassion and caring for others, helping when it is at all possible. This is the most important lesson we have come here to learn, and so has everyone else. The less fortunate also have lessons to learn – perhaps in humility, or in love for others, regardless of circumstances. Every single one of us has lessons to learn and to teach.

And always remember – like everyone else, *you are special*.

Printed in Great Britain
by Amazon

80706974R00079